CURTAIN UP!

John Inman

CURTAIN UP!

Illustrated by
Margaret Chamberlain

Heinemann : London

William Heinemann Ltd
10 Upper Grosvenor Street, London W1X 9PA
LONDON MELBOURNE TORONTO
JOHANNESBURG AUCKLAND

First published 1981

434 94380 0

Printed by
Thomson Litho Ltd, East Kilbride, Scotland

Contents

Foreword

Welcome to the wonderful world of entertainment—from Blackpool. I'm writing this in Blackpool, in my dressing room at the ABC Theatre where I'm appearing in my own summer show, *Fancy Free,* and there really couldn't be a better place to start my first book because this is where it all began for me.

Although I was born in Preston, when I was still quite small my parents moved to Blackpool and opened a guest house. In the back yard of that guest house at the age of five or six I started my career as an entertainer. It was at the end of the Second World War—which, whatever you might think, isn't *that* long ago!—and we used lots of old black-out curtains hung from the clothes line in the yard as stage curtains. And for our shows my friends and I did all the things that you will find in this book, from dressing up and singing songs to putting on plays and making magic.

I didn't turn professional until I was thirteen and then it was only for a fortnight. The Jack Rose Repertory Theatre at the South Pier needed a small boy to appear in a play called *Freda*. Because my school was well known for its annual production of a Gilbert and Sullivan light opera, the people from the theatre came to the school to see if there were any likely lads for the part. Our headmaster, who was a lovely man (he didn't believe in homework or anything like that!), knew I was an idiot and frantic to go on to the stage, so he put me forward for the part. I haven't looked back since.

Between my first amateur appearance in the back yard at the age of five and my first 'professional' appearance on the South Pier at the age of thirteen, I put on hundreds of shows of all sorts for my family and friends, and everything I learned then (and a few things I've learned since) is what you'll find in the pages that follow. I hope you enjoy the book—and, who knows, it may even lead you from your back yard to the ABC Theatre, Blackpool, or even to the bright lights of Broadway! Good luck.

Curtain Up!

There's one thing you have to do when you want to put on a show. It's probably the most difficult part, but only you will know how to do it. What is it? It's starting! It sounds easy, but it isn't. Sometimes *everything* seems a bit of a bore. That's the time to think, well, if I go on sitting here, doing nothing, I'll get more and more bored, but I could be having a good time!

Stir yourself! Don't just think about it—do something! There are lots of ideas in this book to get you going, and, once you have started, you'll discover dozens more.

Your show can have anything in it—songs, jokes, impressions of me being Mr Humphries, even a circus that's as exciting as the one I go to every year under Blackpool Tower, or a fun fair like the one I used to visit as a child in the Market Square in Preston, with a coconut shy, skittles, and a fortune teller. It's up to you! The fun is in thinking up fresh ways of keeping your friends and audience happy.

When you get an idea, think of the best way of presenting it. Ask your granny for costumes, ask your mother for make-up, ask your father for funny

hats. You can use your room as a fairground, or the stairs as part of the stage for your play.

Whatever you do, never forget Inman's Ten Golden Rules for success:

1. *Know what you're doing!*

Before you start, have a clear idea of the sort of show you're going to do. It's no use having a circus-type presentation and then bringing in someone reading poems to fill up a gap. Of course, once you have decided what sort of show you want, invent the right things to perform and have enough of them for twenty minutes, or however long you decide to go on. Know how long your show or play is going to last. If you go through it and it seems to drag, don't be afraid to cut parts out.

2. *Learn and rehearse*

Quite simply, if you do not know your lines, or what you are going to do in your circus ring, or with your puppets, you'll feel like a television newsreader who hasn't been given any news to read. You'll feel terrible, and the show will be a disaster, so learn whatever it is you have to do very thoroughly. Don't try to improvise, at least not until you know the act backwards.

3. *Have a prompt*

A prompter is someone who has a copy of the script and during rehearsals and performances gives the actor his words if he forgets them. Of course, you won't need a prompt, as they're called for short, for your circus, but they're a very good idea for any other show. Your prompt may also be your 'director', telling people what they are doing wrong and how to put it right.

4. *Choose the right props*

'Props' is short for 'properties' and means the bits and pieces you have on stage to help the show. The magician's props would be his wand, his top hat, his pack of cards and whatever else he might need. Whichever kind of show you're doing, a few props will make things more interesting. If you're singing a silly song about eskimoes, wear a fur hat rather than a top hat.

Props help to create the right atmosphere, as well as being a necessary part of the show. Get out the Christmas decorations to jolly up your fairground or your circus ring. Even a simple sing-song might be staged with some funny costumes and a few potted plants around the place.

I used to make all my own props as a boy and, believe it or not, for my pantomimes and summer shows I still do. I think making the props can be almost as much fun as using them. And if you're no good at making things, get your friends to help. I wasn't much good at magic when I was a boy, so my friend made most of the tricks when we put on magic shows in his garage in Preston. Now he runs a business making magic tricks, so when I need a trick for a show I know where to go!

5. *Wear the right clothes*

Costumes make the performance seem real and will give the performers confidence. It's much easier to act like a cowboy if you're dressed like one.

Choosing the right costume can be difficult, and finding all the materials you need sometimes seems impossible, especially when all you have is an old scarf, some wellingtons and a football jersey. If this is the case, you'll have to put treacle on your head and pretend to be a toffee apple—but seriously, have another look round. Ask your mother if you can use things from around the house. Sheets can easily be turned into robes, or ghostly guises. Cushions will make you look fat when you stuff them up your jersey and towels can be made into turbans. Crowns and swords can be made from cardboard, and beards with cotton wool. Keep looking and thinking and you'll find something that will be just right.

Costumes are important and the more you have the merrier. When I'm in pantomime playing the Dame I change my costume fourteen times at every performance!

6. *Look after the audience*

In your fairground the 'public' will look after themselves, but with puppet shows, plays and circus entertainments you'll need to plan the seating so that everyone can see and everyone is comfortable. Ask the tallest people to sit at the back, or to sit cross-legged on the floor. (Your uncle might not like this, so make sure he's got a seat at the back if he's tall!)

7. *What's that noise?*

Your fairground and circus can be bursting with noise but many shows call for complete quiet. If possible, put on your display in a back room, away from street noises. Make sure that anyone not coming to the show keeps quiet. Also make sure that your 'stage'—whatever it's made of—doesn't creak

or squeak, and if you have scenery, see that you can change it quietly between scenes. Building and painting scenery isn't easy (I know because my first real job in the theatre was painting scenery at the New Theatre, Crewe), but it does make your show that much more professional.

8. *Be bright about lighting!*

The ideal time for a play is in the evening. If it's dark, you can light your stage with table lamps placed behind your curtains. If you don't have curtains and the play takes place inside a house, you can put your lamp on a table, so it becomes part of the scenery. If the action takes place outside put your lighting behind a piece of scenery—some cardboard cut into the shape of a rock, for example. When there's some action you wish to highlight, or to which you want to give a mysterious air, you can use a strong torch as a spotlight. You'll need someone to point the torch from the side of the room, or from the side of the stage, but make sure the beam follows the actor smoothly. This will need rehearsal.

9. *Be prepared for the worst!*

A magician once told me that he kept having a terrible nightmare. Every time he tried to pull a rabbit out of his hat, he found that the rabbit had escaped. This never happened to him in real life, but he got so worried that it might, he learnt to stand on his hands, so that if one day his rabbit

disappeared he could get onto his hands and walk off stage in style! If your act goes wrong, you can be like Tommy Cooper and fluff it again on purpose. Whatever happens, don't panic! If you forget your lines in your play, wait for the prompt. For more hints about what to do in a crisis, turn to page 92.

10. *Choose the right time*

Ask your parents or friends when they are free to come to your show. Don't just put it on and expect lots of people to turn up. Check the television programmes to see if there's anything special on—like *Are You Being Served?* If there is, look for a night when there isn't.

Saturday or Sunday afternoons are good times for a circus show or for sing-songs. Generally, though, it's a good idea to put on your shows, especially shadow shows, in the evening when it's dark and you can use artificial lighting to best effect.

And whatever you do and whenever and wherever you put on your show, have fun!

Come to the Concert Party

What is a concert party? Well, it isn't a concert and it isn't a party: it's something in between and it's what I and my friends used to put on in our back yards when we were children.

It's a mixture of music and magic, singing and dancing, a lot of laughs and a few surprises. It's how I began putting on shows at home, and I think it would be a very good way for you to begin as well.

The great thing about a concert party is that it is packed with *variety* so you never give your audience a chance to get bored. By the time they've decided they've had enough of your singing, you're already on to your magic, and the moment they think they've worked out how you do your tricks, you're amazing them with a dazzling display of shadow play.

You'll find all the ingredients for a well-balanced concert party in this chapter. I suggest five different items for your programme: some singing to wake up your audience at the beginning of the show, some magic to amaze them, some music to amuse them, some shadow play to show how different you can be and a rousing chorus of a song everyone knows for a grand finale.

Variety is not just the spice of life: it's what a concert party is all about, so, whatever you do, keep the show moving. Even if you *think* your audience wants more magic than you planned to give them, don't be fooled. Stop each item after five minutes at the most and leave them wanting more!

For a concert party it doesn't much matter what you wear, but do look smart. An audience likes to feel you've taken some trouble with your appearance and if you come on looking bright and lively it will help them feel bright and lively too.

It's just because you want them to feel jolly that it's such a good idea to launch your concert party with a song or two, especially if some of the songs are ones with which they can join in. It'll get the cobwebs out of their lungs and put the audience exactly where they belong: on your side.

Sing Something Simple

When you are going to start with a song and you want the audience to join in, it can help if you have a musical instrument to accompany you, or at least to give you the right note to start on! You might need the help of an adult, though if you play a recorder that will certainly be enough for rehearsals. Perhaps you have an elder brother or sister who can strum a guitar. If they are like my brother Geoffrey—who is a very successful butcher now but was no guitarist when we were young!—turn to the home-made instruments instead. They won't keep you in tune, but they'll add variety to the noise you make!

Always start with a well-known song. With this one, at the end of each verse you make all the noises and sounds that you've sung in every verse up to that point. Your audience can also join in here. You'll see what this means if you look at the song.

She'll Be Coming Round the Mountain

1

She'll be coming round the mountain when she
 comes, (Toot, toot!)
She'll be coming round the mountain when she
 comes, (Toot, toot!)
She'll be coming round the mountain,
She'll be coming round the mountain,
She'll be coming round the mountain when she
 comes! (Toot, toot!)

2

She'll be driving six white horses when she comes,
 (Whoa, back!)
She'll be driving six white horses when she comes,
 (Whoa, back!)
She'll be driving six white horses,
She'll be driving six white horses,
She'll be driving six white horses when she comes!
 (Whoa, back! Toot, toot!)

3

We'll all be there to meet her when she comes, (Hi, there!)
(as before)

4

We'll all eat currant buns when she comes, (Yum, yum!)

5

We'll have to scrub her down when she comes, (Scrub, scrub!)

6

She'll have to sleep with Rover when she comes, (Rruff, rruff!)
She'll have to sleep with Rover when she comes, (Rruff, rruff!)
Oh, she'll have to sleep with Rover,
She'll have to sleep with Rover,
She'll have to sleep with Rover when she comes,
(Rruff, rruff! Scrub, scrub! Yum, yum! Hi there! Whoa, back! Toot, toot!)

After that, if the audience starts shouting, "*Encore! Encore!*" (which is French for "More! More!") you can give them just one more song—but that's their lot. As with your opening song, you sing the verse and let your audience join in the chorus (that's the part in brackets). If you think they may not know the words, get a large sheet of drawing paper and write them in capital letters for everyone to see. Then point at the right words at the time when you want your audience to sing them.

Camptown Races

The Camptown ladies sing this song,
(Doodah! Doodah!)
The Camptown race-track five miles long,
(Oh, Doodah day!)
I come down there with me hat cave in,
(Doodah! Doodah!)
I go back home with a pocket full of tin,
(Oh, Doodah day!
Goin' to run all night!
Goin' to run all day!
I'll bet my money on the bob-tail nag,
Somebody bet on the bay.)
The long-tail filly and the big black hoss,
(Doodah! Doodah!)
They fly the track and they both cut 'cross,
(Oh, Doodah day!)

The Magic Touch

You need a lot of nerve to be a magician so you must know what you're going to do, and leave nothing to chance. All these tricks will work if you have the right props, and the props are everyday things, so you should have no problems in finding them.

Have a table on your stage with your props on it, and check that all your props are there well before the show is due to start.

The tricks here are divided into two parts. The first, called 'The trick', gives you an idea of what to say, and what happens in the trick. 'The secret' tells you how it's done. Here we go then, but remember that practice usually does make perfect. If things go wrong don't worry too much: you're in good company—magic was never my strongest point!

The Banana Trick

(You'll need: 1 banana)

The trick: I have here a very ordinary banana. However, if I say the magic banana-slicing word, 'I'M FREE!' the banana is sliced into ready-to-eat segments! Would someone kindly peel the banana? Here we are, sir! There, what did I tell you? It's neatly cut up—all ready for you to eat!
The secret: If they haven't seen this trick before the audience will be truly amazed but it's quite simple. Before you go on stage you must tamper with the banana. Just get a long needle and pierce one seam of the banana skin. Then, being careful not to slice the skin, wiggle the needle back and forth inside the banana. If you do this at three or four places along the seam, when the banana is peeled it will fall into separate pieces. For the best effect, do not detach it from the bunch, just remember which it is.

Coin and cups

(You'll need: 3 cups, 1 coin)

The trick: On this table, there are three cups and one coin. Now, I'd like someone to come up from the

audience to help me, but not yet! I'm going to go outside and whoever wants to, can come up and hide the coin under one of the cups. Just pick any one you like.

When I come into the room again, everyone must be very quiet, and not move a muscle. It will only take me a moment to work out where the coin is, and I won't touch anything except the cup that covers the coin.

The secret: Although having a helper in the audience isn't something that should happen often, it is very effective if done just once during a performance. As long as your assistant, or accomplice—as he or she ought to be called—doesn't attract any attention, no one will notice what's going on.

When you come back into the room, you must glance at your helper. He will have his forefinger in his mouth. If it's in the middle of his mouth, you must go to the middle cup. If it's in the left side of his mouth, it will be in the cup on your left, and if he's holding his finger on the right side of his mouth the coin will be under the right-hand cup. You must rehearse this well to get used to working out where the coin is, and to make sure you always go straight to the right cup.

Water in the Hand

(You'll need: 1 paper cup, 1 shallow bowl)

The trick: Here I have a paper cup. If you look you can see it's full of water. Can everyone see? Good. Now, this takes nerve, and a steady hand, so I'm going to roll up my sleeves first. Right, now I'll clench my fist, but leave a little hole so I can pour all the water in . . . so! I'll just perform the magic actions and, hey presto! the water's gone!

The secret: The plastic cup actually has a small hole near its base. When you first show the audience the cup full of water, keep your finger over this small hole, which you can make with scissors. When you come to roll up your sleeves, put the cup into the shallow bowl, so that nearly all the water runs out. Then pour the small amount left into your hand. Hold the cup very close to your hand, and pour away from the audience.

The Rolling Cigarette

(You'll need: 1 cigarette)

The trick: Would anyone in the audience happen to have a cigarette? No, I don't want to smoke it, just to perform a little miracle. Thank you. I'll put it on the table here, where you can all see it. Now, I must wet my finger, so, and draw a circle round it. I don't seem to have made it wet enough; I'll lick another finger, and complete the circle. Now I wet this bit, so there's a path towards me and I can transmit the magic energy along it through my finger. When I point my finger at the cigarette, the cigarette will roll away.

The secret: All the business of drawing a circle round the cigarette is, of course, nonsense. The more fuss you make about it, though, the less the audience are likely to realise that you're gently blowing the cigarette away from you when you point your finger. This sounds too simple for anyone to be fooled by, but you just try it. When you blow, remember not to change the shape of your lips, but keep them just a little bit open. Don't have anything else near the cigarette, like a piece of paper, or that will get blown away too, and give the trick away.

The Invisible Thing

(You'll need: 1 brown paper bag)

The trick: I have here a brown paper bag. In my other hand I'm holding an invisible thing. What is it? I don't know. I've never seen it, but it's there all right. You don't believe me? Well, I'll throw it up in the air and catch it in this paper bag. There! But I still don't know what it is!

The secret: This joky trick isn't really magical but it's very funny. Just hold the paper bag so that you can flick its side with your middle finger, having your other two fingers either side, inside the paper bag, and your little finger and thumb free. To make the sound of the 'thing' hitting the bottom of the bag, just flick, using your thumb and middle finger, as if you were flicking away a speck of dust. You can also move the bag downwards a bit, as if the weight of the thing moved it. You can do this two or three times, each time pretending to pick the thing out of the bottom of the bag, and perhaps one of the times you can pretend to miss it, and pick it up off the floor! It's rather a silly trick, but it's a good one with which to end your Magic Moments because it always gets a laugh. And if you don't believe me, ask Eric Morecambe: he's been using it in his act for years!

The Do-It-Yourself Orchestra

No concert party is complete without a musical interlude and a fine concert party orchestra to supply it. If you don't happen to have seventy-six trombones in the broom cupboard and a full symphony orchestra in the garage, it hardly matters. Around the house you'll find all sorts of bits and pieces that you can turn into instruments of your very own.

The Percussion Instruments

Drums and cymbals are essential and you'll find the kitchen is full of them! Do be sure to ask your parents first if you want to borrow anything of theirs, though, because you don't want an angry mum bringing the concert to an abrupt halt to reclaim the giant saucepan that you had planned to use as your big bass drum.

If you find different sizes of saucepans and other interesting 'drums' like a tin teapot, a watering can, some flower pots and even a thick book, you can make a very varied assortment of sounds. The saucepans should be suspended from a line, and

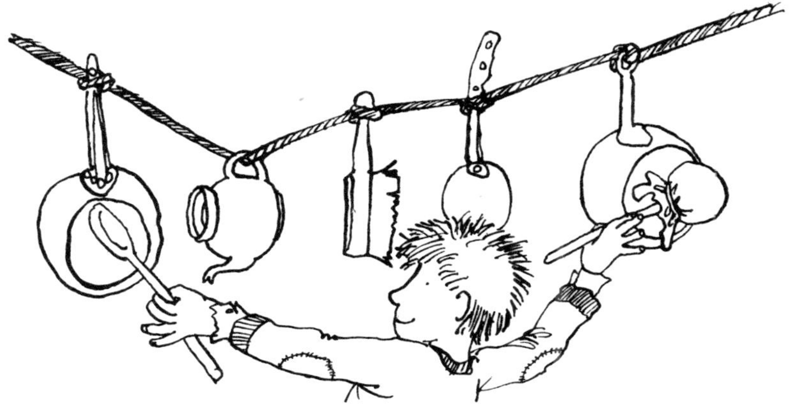

you'll need a drumstick. A wooden stick with half a rubber ball fixed on the end will do quite well, though you can experiment with brush handles, candles, even a wooden spoon or the handle of a screwdriver.

Comb and Paper

This is one of the simplest of all home-made instruments, but, if you can sing in tune, it's one that will give you any tune you know! Just wrap a piece of thin, hard tissue paper round a comb and put the comb lightly against your lips. A sharpish hum produces the best results, but remember to keep the tissue paper tight on the teeth of the comb.

Spoons

Playing the spoons is as difficult as playing a comb and paper is easy. Hold them with their bottoms facing each other, as in the illustration, and then use various parts of your body to knock them against, while singing a popular tune. You'll find that they tend to wobble around so that they miss each other instead of clacking. Keep trying, and you'll find the grip that will keep them in place while you attack various parts of your body!

Washboards

Washboards are quite difficult to find nowadays. If you can't find one in the attic or out in the garage, you might enjoy a visit to some local junk shops to see if they have one. It's worth the effort as washboards produce very good rhythms and are excellent backing instruments for songs like 'Camptown Races'. All you do is put as many thimbles as you have on your right hand and strum away! Thimbles are also getting a bit scarce so ask for them at the junk shop if you haven't any at home.

Wind Instruments

The important thing here is to have an idea of how to blow into anything and get it to make a noise. If this sounds a bit silly, it's really a good way of

producing a great number of different kinds of sounds. You can start with a garden hose. Just purse your lips as if you were going to blow a raspberry, but don't put your tongue out. Now, blow sharply so you get a sort of nose-blowing noise, only through your lips. Once you've mastered this, try it on your hose. It helps if the hose has a smooth end, and isn't too long, so you can hear the note you're making. You can also put a plastic or metal funnel in the other end of the hose, and this will act a bit like the horn on a trumpet.

If this sound isn't to your liking, try any piece of pipe or hose or tubing you can find, though make sure it's clean first. Remember what happened to the old woman who swallowed a spider.

Shadow Shows

In real concert parties (the ones put on at theatres on the ends of piers during the summer holidays) the musical interludes are often rather restful and relaxing. Since yours will be an orchestra of saucepans, combs, washboards and rubber tubing, the music you make will probably be pretty lively! That's why it's a good idea to follow it with a surprise novelty item that will calm your audience down but fascinate them at the same time.

About ten thousand years ago, some cavemen were sitting in a cave in what is now called Maida Vale, in London, not so far from where I now live. They had a big fire going, and they were happily gnawing on some wolf bones when suddenly one of them shrieked in terror, dropped his bone and ran for it. The others laughed when they saw what had happened: a sparrow had got into the cave and flown near the fire. Its shadow was huge, like a Giant Eagle's, and the caveman thought the Big Bird had come to get him. One of the other cavemen, being a bit brighter than the rest, realised that he could make a shadow with his hands, and, like the sparrow near the fire, it would appear much bigger than it really was. Not only that, but he could make shadows that looked like everyday creatures, such as woolly-haired mammoths.

On the next few pages are some easy, and some not-so-easy shadow figures. The best time to try them is when it's dark. Find a light-coloured wall. Ideally, find a white wall without any cracks, picture frames, windows, mirrors or bookshelves. You can't? Well, just get a clean white sheet and pin it up on a wall. (Ask before you stick the pins in; sometimes they cause a lot of damage.) Get a strong torch and put it on a table with its beam facing the sheet. Now, all you have to do is imitate the hand positions as shown in the illustrations.

The Grand Finale

It's time to say goodbye and, like all the best entertainers, you want to go out with a bang. And you will, with a bang on the largest, loudest saucepan in your orchestra. This is the cue for your Grand Finale, a rousing version of 'Old MacDonald's Farm', suitably adapted for you as the star of the show and with a fine orchestral accompaniment. For a full orchestra you really need five friends to play the different instruments, but if you're on your own you can do your best to turn yourself into a one-man band and play the lot yourself!

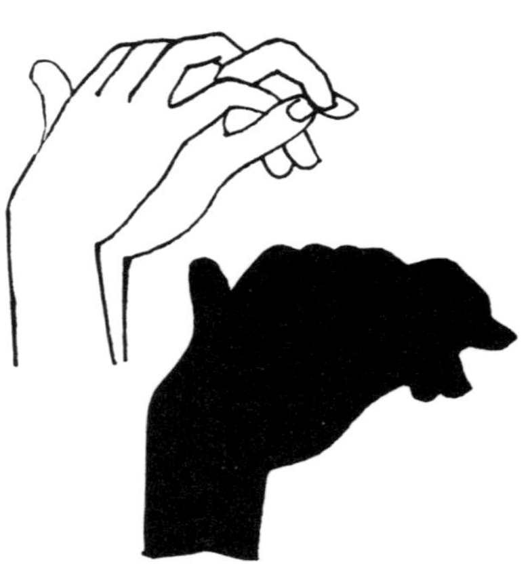

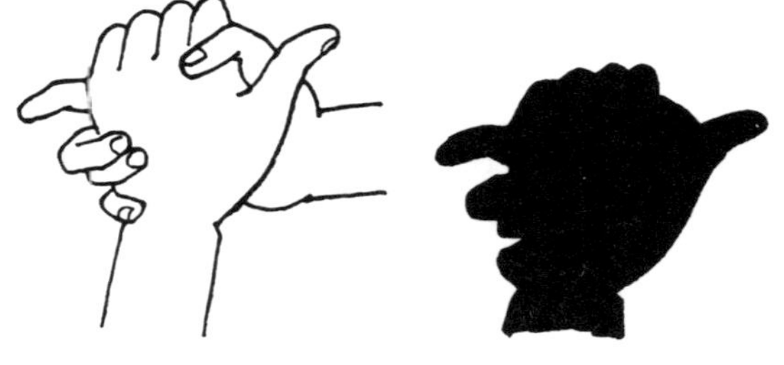

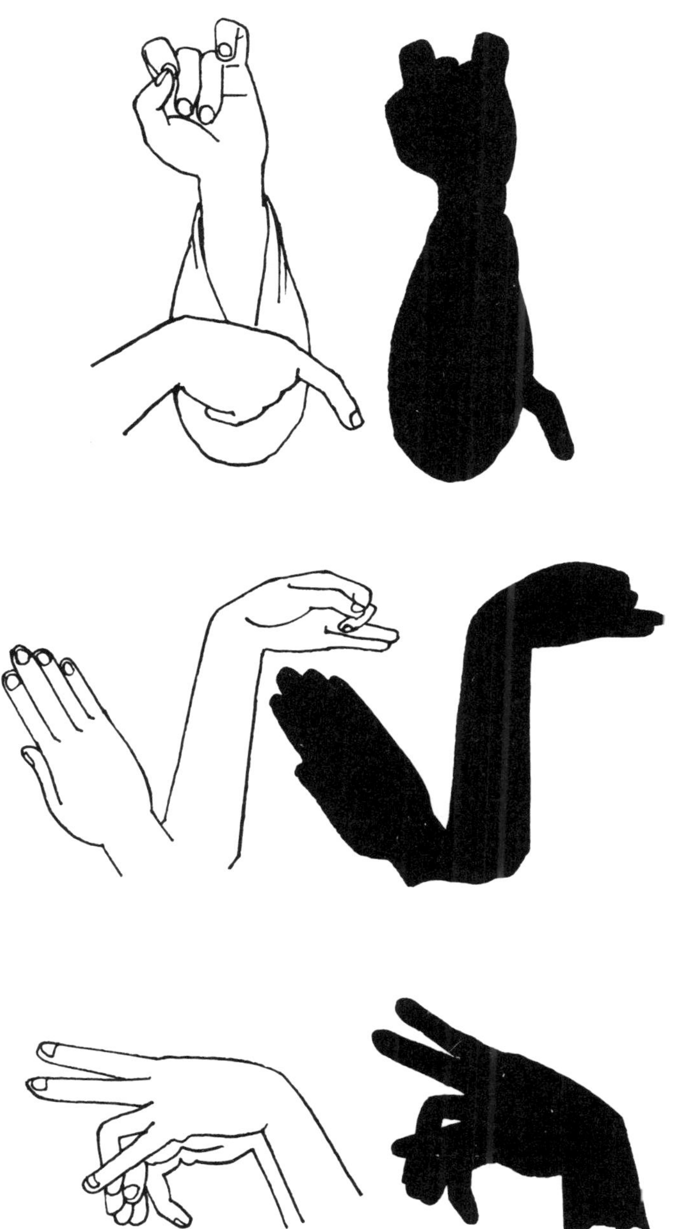

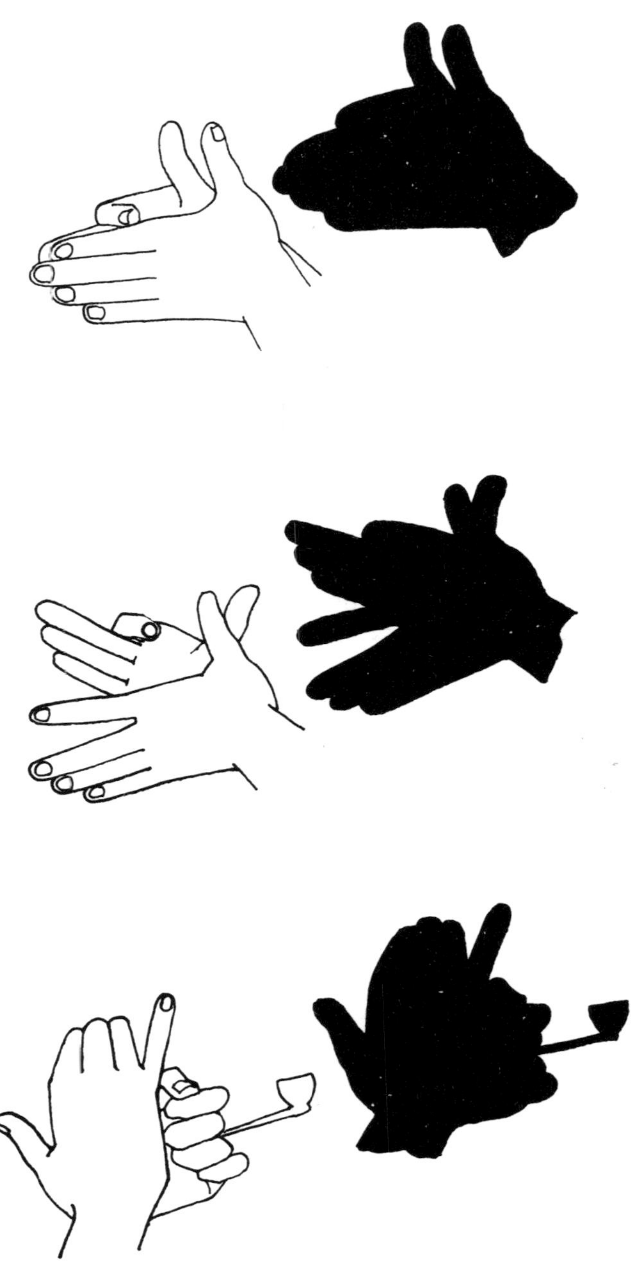

Young John Inman had a shop,
Ee aye ee aye oh,
And in that shop he had some gongs,
Ee aye ee aye oh,
With a (hit saucepans sharply twice) here
And a (hit saucepans sharply twice) there,
Here a (hit saucepan once),
There a (hit saucepan once),
Everywhere a (hit saucepans twice),
Young John Inman had some gongs,
Ee aye ee aye oh!

Young John Inman had a shop,
Ee aye ee aye oh,
And in that shop he had some clocks,
Ee aye ee aye oh,
With a (play spoons) here
And a (spoons) there,
With a (hit saucepans twice) here
And a (hit saucepans twice) there,
Young John Inman had a shop,
Ee aye ee aye oh!

Young John Inman had a shop,
Ee aye ee aye oh,
And in that shop there was a wasp,
Ee aye ee aye oh,
With a (make a wasp noise with
comb and paper) here
And a (do the same again) there,
With a (spoons) here
And a (spoons) there,
With a (hit saucepans) here
And a (hit saucepans) there,
Everywhere a (all the noises
together for some time),

Young John Inman had a shop,
Eeee aye eeee aye ohhhhhh!
(On the last line, play all the instruments
together, as loudly as possible.)

The only other thing I can say is . . . I hope your neighbours are friendly ones!

All the Fun of the Fair

It's one of those days when the rain is coming down. It was raining like this yesterday, and today when the weather man said it was going to be sunny, it's just the same. He said it's going to be sunny tomorrow, so you'd better think of something to do indoors today!

Why not have a fair? But (you say) how do I get the dodg'ems through the door? And where do I get them from? It doesn't have to be *that* sort of fair, of course, because at *that* sort of fair, everything costs a lot of money. At your fair, you can have stalls and sideshows, games with prizes, even a travelling Punch and Judy puppet show.

Ask your parents if you can take over the house for a day. If they say yes, fine! If they say no, ask them how much of the house you can have. I remember as a child that my friends' parents' *garages* were ideal for this, so long as the car wasn't competing with the coconut shy!

Decorate the 'fairground' with as many bright displays as you can. Dig out Christmas decorations and the fairy lights and make your fairground look as lovely and inviting as possible.

You'll want some help setting up the show, so why not ask some of your friends to come along too? It's best if there's one person to each stall or game, and you want as many stalls as possible to make it a big success. You can charge, say, 1p for each go, then use the money as prizes.

Gypsy Rose, the Fortune Teller

Most good fairgrounds have a fortune teller. Although a lot of them are rather less accurate than the weather men, it's good fun to go and hear what they say. Everyone is interested in themselves, so why don't you have a fortune teller to 'tell them their future'?

You need to fix up a small tent, which isn't as hard as it sounds. Ask your mother for an old sheet. Make sure it's long enough to stretch from the ceiling to the ground in whichever room you want to have your fortune teller. Using a corner of the room, pin up the sheet so that it makes a square with the two walls. The bigger the sheet the better as it will give you more room inside the tent. With luck you will have enough room for a very small table and two chairs. In one of the chairs will sit Gypsy Rose, the Wisest Woman in Warrington—or wherever!

To dress as Gypsy Rose you'll need a brightly coloured or spotted head-scarf; some huge ear-rings; a big satiny curtain to drape about yourself; lots of (fake) pearl necklaces and strings of beads, bangles on your wrists and rings for your fingers. If you haven't got all this don't worry. Just wear some dangly things and try to look mysterious.

Inside the tent there won't be much room for decorations, but you might pin up a few weird and wonderful pictures on the wall. If you're very lucky, your mother or father might have a red light bulb somewhere. If you put this in an ordinary table lamp and put the lamp inside the tent everything will look red and eerie.

Now comes the hard part. How do you tell fortunes? Well, first you have to have a crystal ball. This will be difficult to find, but if you have a glass bowl and turn it upside down, it'll do just as well. A goldfish bowl is another possibility, as long as there are no goldfish in it! If you haven't a glass bowl or a goldfish bowl, use an ordinary glass. It's better than nothing.

When your first customer comes in, you ask him to tell you his name, his age and his address. You'll probably know him anyway, so you can gaze into

your crystal ball and say (very seriously), 'Ask me whatever you want to know!' The chances are you'll know the answer or be able to make a very good guess. You must use your imagination a little bit, too. If he asks about the future tell him lots of good news—'You're going to go on holiday and have a really good time', 'You're going to go on a long journey which will bring a lot of good luck'—anything like this. Since it hasn't happened yet, you can't be wrong! You are allowed to make jokes as well, as the idea is just to have some fun. You might say, at the end, '...and someone is going to leave you something big in their will. Let me see, I can see a vague outline...yes, it's very big. It's...an elephant!'

Ten Pence for a Penny

This is a very easy game to set up. Just find a big glass jar. An old sweet jar is ideal and you can get one from a sweet shop for ten pence if you ask nicely. Put a ten pence piece at the bottom in the middle. Now slowly fill the jar with cold water so that the ten pence stays where it is at the bottom of the jar. Find a space in your fairground where the jar can be placed without any risk of it being kicked over. It's a good idea to put it in a tin tub, or

something like that which will take the water if the jar is knocked over. You're now ready for customers.

Tell them that all they must do is cover the ten pence piece with a penny. If they do, they win the ten pence piece! If you're worried about losing a lot of money, just try it yourself—it's *very* difficult.

Skittles

This takes up lots of room. The best place to put it is in a long corridor, but remember that you won't be able to get to the rooms at the end of the corridor if you have a skittle alley in the way!

Find nine empty plastic containers. Old washing-up liquid bottles are the best thing, but you'll have a job finding nine, so you may have to use empty cooking-fat bottles or empty plastic containers which held salt, shampoo or talcum powder. If you haven't enough in your own house, ask your neighbours if they have any.

How to arrange the skittles is up to you. You can have four in the front row, three in the second and two behind, or the other way around, or two in the

front, three in the second and third rows and one at the back.

When he's paid his penny, each player can have three shots at the skittles. Use rubber balls—old tennis balls will do nicely—and keep the scores on a blackboard or a large sheet of paper. If a person's a very good shot, he may knock over all the skittles with his first ball. Put the skittles up again and let him have his other goes, then add the total number of skittles he knocked over together. The person with the highest score at the end of the fair wins all the pennies.

Clothes Peg in a Bottle

Get your customers to stand on a chair and try to drop an ordinary clothes peg into a milk bottle which is on the floor below them. You can let each player have three pegs a go and make the prize for

doing this five pence or more, as it's almost impossible to do—certainly without a lot of practice.

Fishing for Goodies

This stall will take a bit of preparation. The idea is to have a hook on the end of a piece of string and fish out a packet from a big box of packets. The packet may contain a prize or there may be nothing inside!

For your fishing rod use a pencil. If possible get some fishing line, and for a hook use something with a blunt end, such as a shaped paper clip.

Your packages should be all shapes and sizes. The bigger ones should have nothing, or something very small inside, while the smaller ones might have ten pence in. You can stick a small loop of cotton on the outside of each with adhesive tape so that the fishers can get their hooks though. There should be a time limit for fishing, say, thirty seconds.

Spoon the Balloon

To add some action to your fairground, try getting people to spoon the balloon. You provide the balloon and a spoon, and get them to fork out one penny for the pleasure of getting the balloon to the other end of the room and back without it once touching the floor. This will be even more difficult as your fairground fills with visitors. The player can keep the balloon up in the air with taps from the spoon, but is *not* allowed to handle it. If he comes back without once touching it, and without the balloon having touched the floor, he wins a glorious prize—say five pence.

Guess the Number

Put as many marbles as you have in a sweet jar, or a large coffee jar. Each person pays their penny and has a guess as to how many marbles the jar contains. Write down their names, and their guess, then at the end of the fair count the marbles and give a prize to the person who guessed correctly, or who came nearest.

The Puppet Show

No fairground is complete without a puppet show and since the Inman family motto is 'Sock it to 'em, baby!' you had better make your puppets *sock* puppets!

The first thing you've got to do is find some old socks that your parents don't mind your turning into glove puppets. When you have found some, put one on your right hand. It won't look much like a puppet but don't despair. Stick your thumb into its heel, and your fingers into the toe. It is best to put elastic round your wrist to keep the sock tight over your fingers. If you put your thumb against your middle finger, with your fingers pointing at you, you can see the beginnings of a puppet, and imagine the best places for all the bits and pieces you are going to put on.

Mouth

The puppet's mouth is really the palm of your hand and the inside of your thumb and fingers. Try to find a piece of red or pink felt to fit this. Glue the felt to the sock or, if you can sew, stitch it on. Find a scrap of material for the tongue. What kind and colour depends on what sort of creature you want. A friendly creature might have a light pink tongue; a nasty creature might have a purple tongue. If you're making a dragon puppet, give him a long green forked tongue.

Eyes

For the eyes, use small black buttons which will have to be sewed on, or bits of felt. If you stick on

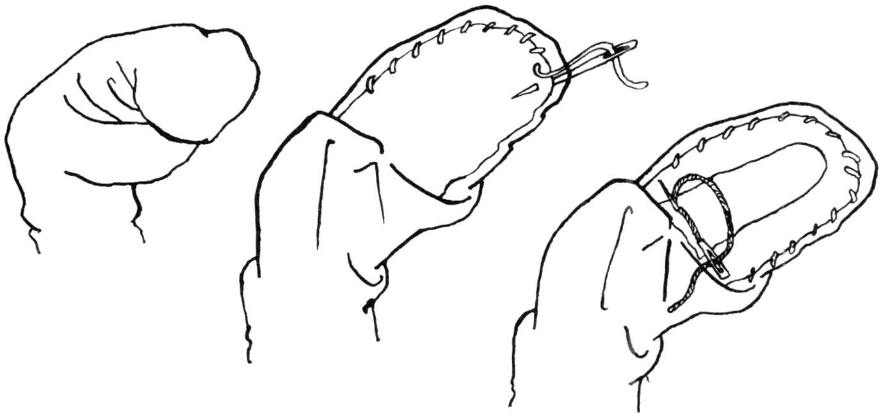

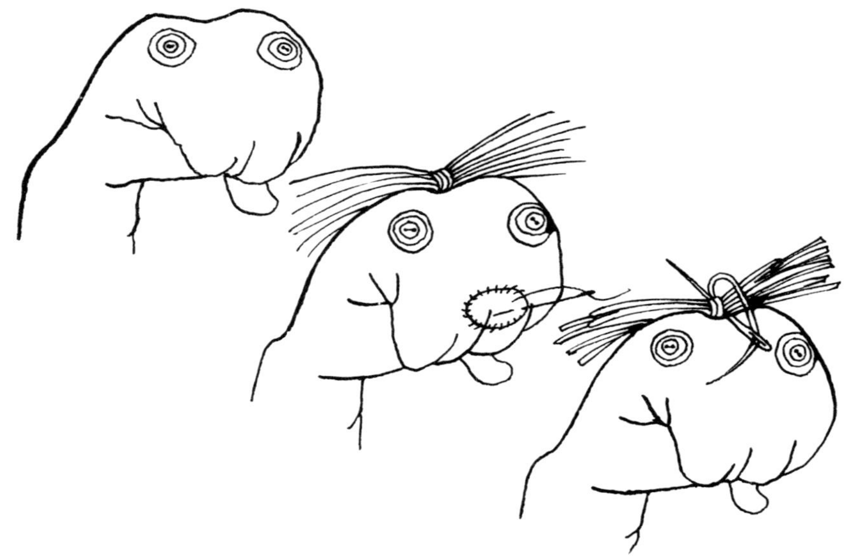

first a piece of white felt, then a circle of blue, then a small circle of black right at the centre, you can make a realistic eye. For monster puppets you can have just the one eye in the centre of the head, but for most puppets put on two, on your knuckles, so that when you bend your fingers to meet your thumb the eyes look straight at you.

Hair

Stick on plenty of wool. If you want hair that flies around use knitting wool; if you want a big mop of hair, use cotton wool.

Nose

The puppet's nose is the end of your fingers. Sew a small black button on, right in the middle of the sock's toe. If you can't sew, or can't get someone to do it for you, glue on a small piece of black cloth.

Your odd sock should now look like... no, not

look like . . . it should *be* an amazing puppet, ready for the stage!

If it's sensitive, and, like me, a bit shy, it might be worried about not having clothes. You can make a little hat out of cardboard and glue it on to the hair. With a long sock that stretches down to your elbow, you can give your puppet a varied wardrobe: for the girl puppets simple dresses made from old scraps of material; for the boys collars made from strips of white paper. Make them ties from long thin pieces of material.

Once you have made your puppets, you'll need a stage, but this can be a very simple thing to make. Find a cardboard box measuring about 45 cm. × 30 cm. The thinner the cardboard the better, as you have to cut out a hole for your stage. Draw a line right round the box, 4 cm. from the edge, and cut along it.

Do not worry if it looks more like a television than a stage; you need to keep the strip at the bottom to hide your hand.

Next, find the oldest and most scratched table in

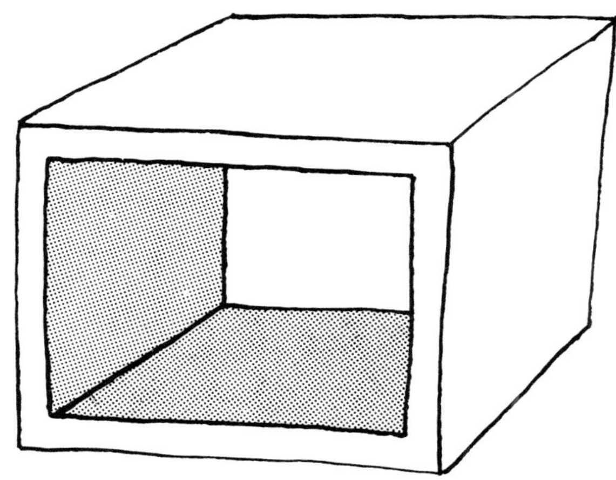

the house. It's a good idea to ask if you can use it. It probably belonged to Aunt Jemima and is now so old that it's worth lots of money! If this is the case, find the second-oldest table. Ideally, it should be quite narrow and quite high.

Put a big cloth over the table, seeing that the cloth reaches the floor all the way round.

Now you can get your theatre ready for the performance. Make curtains from pieces of red velvet or any red cloth you can find in your house. Glue them inside so they hang down at the sides of the stage. You can tie them back with pieces of cotton and use sticky tape to stick the ends of the cotton to the inside of the frame.

Colour the outside of the box and, if you think you can, put on some designs and shapes. You can also make a 'roof' for your theatre. This can be one flat piece of cardboard cut into a triangle and stuck against the front of the box at the top. Again, this can be coloured and have designs on it.

Place your theatre on the back of your table, on the cloth, and fix it to the table with drawing pins. (Don't forget to ask your parents first.) Put the pins on the inside, with their tops digging into the cardboard, all round the inside.

For the performance you kneel or sit on a low stool behind the table, so that only puppets show in the theatre.

Once you have made your puppets and built your theatre, you've got to put on your puppet show. You can make up a story of your own or you can present the show everyone quite rightly expects at a fairground: *Punch and Judy*. It is an old story and one that puppeteers have been putting on at village fairs for hundreds of years. This is how it goes, or at

GLUE
GLUE

least how it used to go when I saw it first on the beach at Blackpool.

Judy tells Punch that she is going out shopping, and that he must look after the baby while she's out. (For the baby, you can use a small bundle of clothing on a tiny table on your stage. When Punch comes to throw the baby out of the window, he can pick it up with his teeth—it will make the story even more dramatic.) She goes out and soon the baby starts crying. Punch tries to sing to it, but it cries louder. He gets angry and shouts at it. It cries louder still. (You can get your friend to do the baby's crying and yowling.) At last, he hits it, and when it's howling, he gets so angry he picks it up and drops it out of the window.

Judy comes back. She is furious when she finds out what's happened. She hits Punch, but Punch hits back and kills her. A policeman comes, but Punch escapes. While he is trying to keep out of the policeman's hands he meets other characters. Usually these include a crocodile and a doctor, but he can meet any of the puppets you've made—a dragon, or a monster, or a ghost—and fight them. He kills each one, but soon the policeman catches him, and he is carried off to prison.

Punch stays on stage all the time, so make the actions dramatic, and don't worry if it all seems a bit silly: it should look funny to your audience.

You might have a job making the policeman look like a real policeman. You can get over this simply by making the policeman-puppet say, when he first appears, 'I'm a policeman, and I've come to arrest you!' Punch says, 'You don't look like a policeman.' The policeman replies, 'Well, I was having a bath when your neighbours called me, and when I went

Judy
POLICE

to get my uniform, I found it had been stolen!'

The lovely part about having your own fun fair at home is that you can keep it going all afternoon long, with people having as many turns at the different side-shows as they want. Of course, your puppet show is the main attraction so put that on at a set time and insist that everyone comes to watch—otherwise you'll find half your audience are bouncing balloons when they should be watching Punch bounce the baby!

Circus Time

Roll Up! Roll Up!

My favourite circus is the permanent one at the foot of the famous Blackpool Tower. Whenever I'm in Blackpool, I visit it and have a wonderful time. Except in Blackpool and London and a few other big cities, the circus doesn't come to town all that often. Of course, that needn't worry you because *you* can put on your own circus at home! Naturally, your mother might get a little upset if she came into the house one day and found you with your head in a lion's mouth. She would probably say, 'John, *stop* teasing that poor lion AT ONCE!' Well, it *is* quite difficult getting elephants and horses through doors, so what you've got to do is create your own rather special circus the Inman way.

The Ring

Let's begin at the beginning. You'll need a ring for your show. This calls for a big room, so ask if you can have the biggest room in the house for an afternoon. Ask well in advance so your parents

don't get alarmed when you start emptying the room of its furniture. You can tell them what you're going to do; they might even have some good ideas of their own!

Once the room is clear of everything except chairs, arrange the chairs in a semi-circle near the walls. You'll need to use the door of the room as your entrance and exit, so have this at the back of what is to be your arena. You can decorate the walls with posters and flags and banners which say something like:

John Inman proudly presents
THE FANCY FREE FAMILY CIRCUS

Every circus has its band. If you don't want to use your do-it-yourself orchestra (because all the musicians are already appearing in the circus as clowns and acrobats!) get just one friend to be the musical director and equip him with a radio or a cassette player or a record player, or even get him to hum, whenever you need music. He or she doesn't have to be in the same room; you can put your musical director outside and keep the door open.

The Show

The show should be divided into different 'acts' or 'turns' with all the variety and pace for which your concert parties are now famous. For example, they could range in quick succession from some clowns having a pillow fight to a group of acrobats tumbling. Before you begin to rehearse for your circus, decide which acts you can do, and how many you are going to have. If each act lasts about four minutes, you might think it's a good idea to have five altogether. The whole show would then last about twenty-five minutes, if you include the time it takes to get in and out of the arena, with compèring from the ring-master.

As with a play, you need to rehearse a lot to be able to put on a good show. Have a circus director, and obey him or her! (Now I'm a professional actor I *always* obey my director—well, *almost* always!) If you're the director make sure the space you rehearse in is about the same size as the one in which you are going to perform the show.

You need to rehearse not only what you are going to do in the arena, but also entering and going off again. You're on-stage the moment you come through the door, so you need to be doing something as you cross the floor to the centre of your arena. This can be a little bow to the audience, or if you're clowning, start as soon as anyone can see you.

If anything goes wrong, pretend it hasn't, and carry on with whatever comes next!

The Ring-Master

The person in charge of the circus—in your case your director—is also the ring-master. He welcomes everyone to the circus and does most of the introductions to the different 'acts', most, but not all. It's an amusing idea to have one of the clowns acting as an 'assistant ring-master' and helping out with the introductions in a daft way. As the show goes on, the clown can make more and more fun of the ring-master, who gets so annoyed at the end that he chases the clown out of the ring.

The ring-master proper should be dressed very smartly, wearing a bow-tie. His hair should be very well brushed, and he should gleam with brightness. To the sound of music, he jogs into the centre of the ring, stops sharply and says,

> 'Good evening, ladies and gentlemen, and welcome! Tonight we bring you the most spectacular, the most stunning, the most splendiferous show on earth! Not only clowns, but a performing dog! Not only a

performing dog, but a performing horse! Sit back and enjoy the fun, the acrobats, the daring displays in . . . The Fancy Free Family Circus!'

Just as he finishes speaking, the first act should come into the arena.

The Clowns

The funniest clown I ever saw was the late, great Charlie Carioli. He was a genius! I love all clowns and you will find that lots of your friends will want to play the part of the clown in your circus. Let them, so long as each one makes his or her own costume.

You can try out your own ideas for clown costumes, but this is *my* favourite and it's a perfect clown costume for a boy or a girl to wear.

Starting at the bottom, the costume is made up of very long shoes. You'll have to borrow your father's shoes, stuff up the spare space with newspaper, and tie them to your feet! If you decide to have a lot of action in the show, some of you or all of you can wear ordinary pumps or sneakers, otherwise there'll be tears and broken ankles.

Next, find a pair of very baggy trousers. Don't worry if they're much too wide at the waist and too long in the leg—this is just how they should be. Roll up the bottoms until they're a little way from your shoes. Now you have to find some braces. Your father might have some, but if he hasn't you can soon create your own. Take two lengths of ribbon that will stretch from the top of the trousers, over your shoulder and down your back, like ordinary braces. As you can see from the picture, the ribbons cross at the back, but they go straight down the front. They're held in place with safety pins.

For a clown's shirt, ask your father if he has any very old stripy shirts. If he hasn't, wear a stripy or bright T-shirt. In either case, wear a very old tie, loosely knotted.

Clowns' faces have a lot of white on them. The easiest way of making your face white is to cover it in talcum powder. Don't use toothpaste; it's stronger than you think and will make your eyes run! Once you're white and smelling sweet, you can put eye-shadow round your eyes, and above and below draw two short lines to make your eyes look starry.

For a nose, get half an egg-shell, wash it well but carefully, and stick it to your nose with a piece of clear sticky tape. The tape should go from the top of your nose down. You might like to have a jolly red nose. Ask your mother if you can borrow some nail varnish. Paint the shell with the varnish and wait for it to dry.

You can give yourself big, red lips, too, using red lipstick. Don't be afraid to colour beyond your lips; it will come off with soap and water after the show.

To make a clown's hair, get a friend to hold his hands out in front of him, and a little way apart. Wind yarn round his hands until it looks as if you have enough for a big mop, then tie it round the middle with the end of the yarn. You can now cut each end and you will have a nice woolly wig to wear. Hold it on your head with a few well-placed hair-pins. These will hold the wig to your real hair, and you'll be able to shake it about without it flying off.

The Acts

The clowns will be the stars of your show. There are two good reasons for this. First, clowns are very popular and everyone enjoys seeing them. Second, there aren't an awful lot of things you can do without lots of equipment or large wild animals. Pack your circus with lots of funny acts, and don't worry about missing out the serious or dangerous ones.

While the ring-master is finishing his little speech, the clowns can run on stage and begin their act. What the clowns do doesn't matter much, so long as they make the audience laugh. You might begin by getting the clowns to tell a joke each and then have them pick a fight. Clown ONE can trick Clown

TWO into turning round, then ONE kicks TWO's backside. TWO can get ONE to walk forward, then try to trip him up (be careful!). There should be lots of shouting, and cries of pain when either gets hurt. When they have their feet trodden on, they can hop about on one leg until they have the other one trodden on, then they try to hop with both legs, then fall over, then get up again to do the same to the other clown. Keep it simple, with lots of noise and action.

After the clowns you might have someone who is good at cartwheels and the things that acrobats usually do in the circus ring. You shouldn't perform on a wooden floor as you're likely to pick up large splinters, nor should you throw yourself around on tiles as you'll probably knock yourself out if you have an accident! If there isn't a carpet in the room you have chosen, you must get one in there somehow.

The acrobat can do whatever he or she can: some cartwheels, a handstand, the splits, some walking on hands, making a bridge or twirling like a ballet dancer. It may be difficult to do enough things for an act of five minutes, so the clowns should come on and try to imitate whatever the acrobat did. They fail, of course, and fall over each other at the same time which sparks off another argument. When the acrobat has gone through the act for a second time with the clowns trying to imitate each move, he should finish—if he can—by walking off-stage on his hands. If he can't do this, he should move to the door just before doing his last display of acrobatics, say it's the splits, and take a bow and go off. The clowns can fail even worse than before, and stagger off, clutching their aching bodies.

Do you have a dog? If you do, and it's an obedient dog, it can probably take part in your show.

Have someone who knows the dog well bring him on. He can be on a lead for a little while. Ask the dog to do whatever he can—sit, lie down, roll over, get up, beg, or play dead. Some dogs can close doors, or throw food off their noses into the air and catch it in their mouths. Of course, if you want your dog to do anything as clever as this, you'll have to start training him a long time before your circus! The main thing is to have the dog in the ring for just a short while. It can be for a minute, or even less, and then let him off his lead. He'll probably go over and sit down with the audience, and you can go straight on with your next act.

If you turn to page **68** you'll see how to dress up as a pantomime horse. After the dog has performed,

bring on the horse! It should scamper out and to the front of the arena, bend one knee and bow its cardboard head. Then a clown comes on with a football and throws the ball for the horse to balance on its head. Each time, it misses completely. The clown shouts at the horse, 'You're supposed to balance it on your *head*!' and gets more and more angry. The horse skips around not trying. At last, when the clown gets very angry, the horse goes after the ball and plays football with it, passing it to its back two legs as soon as the clown tries to get it.

When all the acts have been seen—and applauded!—and both the audience and the performers are exhausted but happy, the ring-master brings everybody into the ring and they parade around it three times, waving goodbye!

Time To Dress Up

I have always adored dressing up. Nowadays, when I appear in a pantomime or a spectacular summer show, I have special costumes made for me, but when I was a boy I just raided my mother's old clothes box and dressed up in whatever I could find.

A Silly Fashion Show

You can have a lot of fun simply dressing up in old clothes, so long as they aren't your own and don't fit you properly! To organise a Silly Fashion Show get each of your friends to dress up in the most ridiculous things they can find, but be sure you all check with your parents before you start ransacking drawers and cupboards. Put on old skirts and shirts and scarves and hats and gumboots, and line up for the benefit of the adults. Ask them to decide who looks silliest.

Costume Parade

If you want to be more organised and dress up as a particular character, that shouldn't present too many problems either. Here are my favourite disguises for you to try and, as you'll see, they're all easy to make and suitable for boys or girls. In fact, if we ever bump into each other you may not recognise me. You certainly won't, I hope, when I'm disguised as Frankenstein's Monster.

Frankenstein's Monster

It was about seven feet tall, so you'll have trouble being quite as big, but you can make yourself look big by wearing an old dark jacket that's too small for you, and by having your shirt sleeves rolled up inside your jacket sleeves. It's best if your shirt is without a collar, so if you have a shirt that has been put into the jumble pile, retrieve it, take off the collar and wear that. Your trousers should be dark-coloured, and too small, and you should wear heavy

black boots on your feet. If you can't find a pair, just wear your wellingtons with your trousers over their tops.

Your face make-up should be very dramatic. You need black cracks on your forehead, green cheeks and bright red lips. If you have got your own make-up or special face paints, you're in luck. If you haven't, ask your mother if she has any old make-up you can borrow. As a last resort, use felt-tip pens. Be warned: they do the job well, but the ink takes a lot of washing to get off!

Ghost

Everyone should be able to dress up as a ghost. Just find a big white sheet, put it over yourself and make ghostly noises. What's a ghostly noise? That's a difficult question. Very few people have ever heard a ghost, but they're supposed to make a noise that's something like an owl when it's falling downstairs—oooo—aaaarghhh! But be careful if you have anyone in your family who's very nervous!

If you can find a sheet that's old enough, ask your mother if you can have it 'for keeps' or to give back to her for dusters. Then you can cut eye-holes and see where you're going when you've got the sheet on. You can also ink in a nasty black nose and a grinning mouth, using a felt-tip pen. Wear a circle of elastic as a headband to keep the sheet in place.

Jockey

A jockey's costume may seem an unusual choice but don't forget you will probably need someone to ride your horse in the circus. For the boots, get out your wellingtons and give them a good wash. If you have

any jodhpurs, wear them, and wear a stripy football shirt. If you haven't got these, wear baggy trousers and an ordinary shirt, and roll the sleeves right up. Pin a large number to your front and back. Borrow a flat cap from your father, and wear it sideways so the peak is pulled down over your ear. For a whip, find a bendy, thin, stick, and carry it like jockeys usually carry theirs, sometimes taking swipes at bits of fluff that happen to be in your way!

Chef

Chefs are often quite plump; their cooking is so good, they can't resist trying their food! You can put some cushions up your pullover to make yourself look fat. Wear a white apron, if you have one, or a white shirt and light trousers. To make a chef's hat, find a big white paper bag that fits over your head, and roll the top down a little way.

Artist

Artists often wear something called a 'smock'. This is like a shirt, but you put it on over your head, and it has a pocket right along the front at the bottom. You might be able to find one, but if not, wear the oldest shirt and trousers you can find and flick paint on them, or colour them with watercolours. You'll also need a palette. This is a flat board used by artists on which they mix colours. It often has a hole in it for the thumb to go through so it can be held easily in one hand. You can make one out of cardboard and again paint different colours on it to make it look used. Put a small paintbrush behind your ear, and carry two or three in your right hand. As a finishing touch, you might wear a beret with the side pulled down to your ear.

Robot

You'll need plenty of cardboard boxes to make yourself look like a robot. Find two medium-sized ones for each arm, making holes through them so they fit comfortably, but don't slip. Get a big one for your chest. Cut a hole in the top for your head to go through, and two holes for your arms. Lastly, find a box for your head and paint a robot face on it.

Wear tights on your legs and walk jerkily, moving your head to the left and right, and talk like a Dalek!

Pantomime Horse

The only time my brother Geoffrey and I appeared in any kind of show together was when we were both in *Mother Goose* at the Claremont Congregational Church Hall. Geoffrey, who was about

fourteen at the time, was the goose—and a very good goose he made too. I think he might have been great as the front end of a pantomime horse as well, but after his triumph in feathers he retired from the stage for ever.

If you're going to put on a pantomime at home (see page 74) or have a horse in your circus (see page 63), you'll need a good horse costume, and you'll also need *two* people to play the one part. The back person hangs on to the sides of the front person's trousers, keeping his head down so that his back is the back of the horse. The front person is the horse's neck and head.

When you are both in position, wrap yourselves in a sheet, leaving just your legs and the front person's head free. Don't wrap the sheet too tightly, especially round the person at the back: he must be able to breathe freely. You'll need someone to help you finish off the wrapping and to fix a tail at your back end. The tail can be a few lengths of knitting wool knotted together at one end and pinned on with a safety pin.

For a head, find a long thin cardboard box, the same width as your own head. Cut a hole in one side, near the top, for your head. The open end of the box, if there is one, should be at the bottom. Make two pointed ears from cardboard and stick them on the top corners of the box where you'd expect to find horses' ears. Draw eyes on the sides of the box.

When you perform make sure there's plenty of space so that you don't knock things over. You'll need to practise walking together in a straight line, turning and backing. It's quite a challenge!

Make-Up

You can use your imagination and have a lot of fun experimenting with make-up. You can ask your mother what make-up she uses, and whether you can try some of it. First, think of who or what you want to look like. You might want to look like a red-faced farmer. Use some red lipstick and put a little on both cheeks. Rub this so that it spreads across your cheek, making you look like a ripe apple. With the rest of the costume—wellington boots, and straw in your hair—you need very little make-up to look something like the real thing!

It is very difficult to look old. For my very first part as a professional actor I had to play a man of sixty-five and making the make-up look realistic wasn't easy! Young actors often find they have to make up to look old and older actors often want to make up to look younger, which is sometimes even more difficult!

A somewhat messy (but enjoyable) way of making your face look very different as well as very old requires a spoonful of syrup from the kitchen as its basis. If you make a mixture of syrup and water in a bowl, you'll have a sticky liquid which will keep bits of whatever you want on your face. Cover your whole face with this sticky stuff, and before it has dried, put on sheets of pink, soft toilet tissue. Keep your face straight while this is drying (it's a good idea to be by yourself!), but once it is dry, you can frown and laugh to crease your skin. You will look very different from usual, and you can use your mother's make-up to improve things further.

Using eye-shadow (or special face paints) put heavy lines under your eyes, and mark the lines running down your face from your nose to your mouth. Put about three lines across your forehead as well.

To get the mess off, wash carefully with warm water and soap. Don't clog the drain up with bits of wet tissue, but put them into a bin or into the toilet.

If you don't want to look old but you do want to look *different*, you can change the shape of your face by putting small lumps of cotton wool between your gums and your cheeks, and you can black out one or more of your front teeth with black crayon to look as though you have some teeth missing.

You can buy very grand false beards and moustaches, but they are expensive, difficult to glue into position and take quite a time to get off. You can make your own false moustache by using strands of brown or black wool, taped together in the middle with scotch tape and then glued to your top lip. To make a false beard get two pieces of string, one to stretch from ear to ear, and one to make a hole for your mouth. Tie them together (see p 71), with loops to go round your ears.

Now get a roll of cotton wool and cut out the shape you want for your beard. Glue the beard to the string.

You can wear the beard as it is if you want a white one. If you don't, paint the cotton wool the colour you want with poster paints. Wait until the paint has dried and your beard will be ready.

Once you and all your friends have found costumes and dressed yourselves and made yourselves up, you can have a grand costume parade for the enjoyment of anyone who wants to come and see you in disguise. Perhaps your parents would give a small prize for whoever they think is wearing the best costume, if they can work out who that person really is!

Showtime

Putting on a play at home isn't easy, but it is enormous fun and worth the time it takes to do. The secret is keep things simple! Don't go in for a lot of scenery and props—choose a play with a good storyline, a few jokes and some action, and forget the frills!

You might have written a play yourself. Why not put it on? Don't be shy about asking your friends to take part, but if they make jokes about your play, ask them how they would do it, and write down their ideas.

If the play is your own, you will probably act as director. Directors are often seen as romantic or powerful figures, telling everyone what to do and going for huge lunches in enormous cars. If this is how you want to be, the best thing is for someone else to direct the play; you'll only ruin it. In reality, the good director knows what he wants, but listens to the actors' suggestions. He doesn't ever lose his temper, or throw his hands in the air and say, 'Oh, I give up!', or shout at everyone and walk off.

A perfect director is tolerant, patient, wise, encouraging, modest and *never* throws tomatoes during rehearsals!

If you'd like to be a director and put on a play at home, but you don't happen to have written a play yourself, don't worry: I've got one for you here. It's the pantomime *Cinderella*. I have appeared in it so many times I've lost count. It's probably the most popular of all pantomime stories and it is certainly one of my favourites. In this version, you only need five or six people to act all the parts.

CINDERELLA
BUTTERCUP } her ugly sisters
DAISY }
BUTTONS
PRINCE CHARMING
THE FAIRY GODMOTHER

If you have only got five actors, any one of them (apart from the person playing Cinderella) can double up and play the Fairy Godmother as well. If you have eight people who want to take part, you can bring on your pantomime horse at the end of Scene One and it can lead Cinderella off to the Prince's ball.

While Buttons ought to be acted by a boy and Cinderella and the Fairy Godmother ought to be acted by girls, the parts of the Prince and the two

Ugly Sisters can be played by boys *or* girls. In fact one of the old pantomime traditions is that the hero, who is called the Principal Boy (here Prince Charming), is played by a girl actress dressed up as a boy, and the laughable old lady, who is called the Dame (in this case there are two dames: the Ugly Sisters), is played by a man dressed up like a woman. When I appeared in *Cinderella* I was always one of the Ugly Sisters and my old friend Barry Howard was the other. We had a lot of fun—and so will you!

If you want to put on this pantomime at home, you must read it through several times before you start and work out all the moves. You must make sure that everyone learns their lines and have lots of rehearsals before you put on a public performance.

You won't need much scenery. In fact, for the kitchen at Stonybroke Hall you only *need* a chair, but you can add all sorts of extra bits and pieces as well. A table, a fireplace, a broom for Cinderella, some pots and pans, a pumpkin in the corner, will all help make the scene look more real. For the ballroom at the palace, you don't really need any scenery at all, but it is important that you get someone to ring a bell or make a noise that will sound like a clock striking twelve.

The costumes are easy too. You can make them as grand or as simple as you like. Cinderella should wear a simple skirt to begin with and a pretty party dress when she goes to the ball. The Ugly Sisters should look as ridiculous as possible, the Prince as smart as he can and Buttons can wear something simple (like a boiler-suit) throughout. The Fairy Godmother should wear a pretty dress and, if possible, a pair of fairy wings.

John Inman proudly presents

CINDERELLA

A Potted Pantomime in Three Scenes

Scene One: THE KITCHEN AT STONYBROKE HALL

(*Cinderella is discovered sitting by the fireside looking miserable.*)

CINDERELLA: Oh dear, I'm so unhappy and I don't know what to do. My sisters, Buttercup and Daisy, are so cruel to me. They make me work all day and half the night. I have to get up before five in the morning to start my chores. I've got to do everything for them—wash their clothes, polish their shoes, clean their rooms, cook their meals. I wouldn't mind, but they're always so rude to me as well. If Father was here he'd put a stop to it, but ever since Mother died he's been up in town trying to make enough money to keep his daughters in style. When I'm not working, I just sit here in my rags by the fire, crying a little and dreaming about the fairy-tale prince who will one day come and ask me to be his wife. But it's just a dream and I know I'm going to spend the rest of my life here, all alone. I've got nothing and no one.

(*Buttons has just come in.*)

BUTTONS: You've got me!

CINDERELLA: Of course, I have Buttons! How could I ever forget you?

BUTTONS: I'm pleased to hear you say that, Miss Cinders, because I'm your friend you know. In fact, I think I'm the only friend you've got.

CINDERELLA: That's true, Buttons.

BUTTONS: And, by Jiminy, you need a friend, living here all on your own with those two battle-axes.

CINDERELLA: Really, Buttons, you mustn't call them that! They are my sisters, after all.

BUTTONS: They're not very sisterly sisters if you ask me.

CINDERELLA: Now, don't be naughty.

BUTTONS: And why not, may I ask? I think you're too good to them. You shouldn't put up with them. I know I'm only the skivvy round here. I know I don't count for anything, but take my advice, Cinders. Stand up to those two. Tell them what you think of them. Be firm. Be positive. They're a couple of nasty old frumps and it's high time you came out and said so.

BUTTERCUP: CINDERELLA!

(*off-stage*)

BUTTONS: Oh, crikey, here they come! I'm off.

(*Buttons goes off to the right and Buttercup and Daisy, the Ugly Sisters, come in from the left.*)

BUTTERCUP: Ah, Cinderella, here you are.

DAISY: Sitting around doing nothing as usual, I see.

BUTTERCUP: Lazy child.

CINDERELLA: Oh, sisters, I'm so sorry. I was only taking a little rest before making the supper.

DAISY: 'A little rest'! You must be joking! What does a strapping great horse of a girl like you need with a 'little rest'?

CINDERELLA: Oh, I hope I'm not a strapping great horse of a girl.

BUTTERCUP: Of course you are, child. Now don't take offence. The truth never hurt anybody.

DAISY: Don't think we blame you. It's not your fault you're as plain as a pineapple and as simple as a sardine.

BUTTERCUP: Just as it's not our fault that we're the greatest beauties for miles around.

DAISY: I wouldn't say 'we' if I were you. I think it is generally acknowledged that I am the greatest beauty in this part of the kingdom.

BUTTERCUP: Rubbish! You're not bad for your age but when it comes to true beauty, you can't beat the real thing.

DAISY: True beauty? Tush! Mutton dressed up as lamb.

CINDERELLA: Sisters, sisters, don't fight.

BUTTERCUP: You're right, child, it's not right to have fights within the family. Besides my health can't take it. I'm such a delicate thing.

DAISY: Delicate! My foot!

CINDERELLA: Now don't start all over again.

BUTTERCUP: Yes, don't start all over again. At the

best of times I'm weak, but after this morning's breakfast I feel as if I'm knocking at death's door.

CINDERELLA: Was something wrong with breakfast?

BUTTERCUP: Wrong? My dear child, you were never a good cook, but today you excelled yourself. As you know, I like my eggs boiled for precisely three minutes, not a second more, not a second less. Today my eggs must have been boiled for at least three minutes and a half. It isn't good enough.

DAISY: No, it really isn't. Your standards are dropping, girl. I think we'll have to teach you a lesson. You'll get no wages this week.

CINDERELLA: But I don't get any wages anyway.

BUTTERCUP: Quite right too.

DAISY: If we had our way, you'd pay us for the privilege of living in such charming company.

CINDERELLA: But I'm your sister.

DAISY: Yes, aren't you lucky!

CINDERELLA: Oh sisters, I promise I'll try to be better in future.

BUTTERCUP: That's more like it. Well, you can get cracking right away and give me something to drink.

DAISY: I feel just like a cup of tea.

(*Buttons enters.*)

BUTTONS: That's right—sloppy, wet and hot!

DAISY: You cheeky brat. How dare you speak to me like that?

BUTTERCUP: What are you doing in here, anyway?

BUTTONS: I've come to tell you that there's a fellow at the door who wants to come in.

DAISY: It'll be the police!

BUTTERCUP: No, it won't, it'll be the tax collector.

CINDERELLA: It isn't someone with news from Father, is it?

BUTTONS: No, it's a fellow called Dandini. He says he's Prince Charming's valet!

CINDERELLA:
BUTTERCUP:
DAISY: } Prince Charming's valet.

BUTTERCUP: Show him in, show him in.

DAISY: At last, at last, the moment I've been waiting for.

BUTTERCUP: What do you mean, the moment you've been waiting for.

DAISY: Well, the Prince has obviously seen my picture in the local paper and decided *I'm* the one who should be his bride. He's looking for a wife you know.

BUTTERCUP: I know he's looking for a wife, but he's not looking for you. He could go to the zoo if he wanted to see the likes of you. It's the likes of *me* he's after!

DAISY: Poppycock!

BUTTERCUP: How dare you! I'll tear your eyes out!

(*They are at each other's throats, when Buttons, who had gone to fetch Dandini, returns.*)

BUTTONS: Prince Charming's valet.

(*Enter Prince Charming, disguised as Dandini. He bows to the Ugly Sisters, but doesn't notice Cinderella who is hidden behind them.*)

CINDERELLA (*aside*): This is the Prince of my dreams! Can it be true?

PRINCE: Ladies this is indeed a pleasure.

BUTTERCUP: You're too kind, I'm sure, Mr. Bebeano.

PRINCE: Dandini's the name, madam.

DAISY: Of course it is, I knew that. Ignore her, your valetship.

PRINCE: Let me get straight down to business.

BUTTERCUP: }
DAISY: } Yes, yes?

PRINCE: I am here on behalf of His Highness, Prince Charming.

BUTTERCUP: }
DAISY: } Yes, yes?

PRINCE: To invite you . . .

BUTTERCUP: }
DAISY: } To be his ever-loving wife!

PRINCE: Not at all, far from it. Whatever put that idea into your heads?

BUTTERCUP: I'm so sorry, to be sure.

DAISY: Carry on, carry on.

PRINCE: To invite you to his grand ball which is being given at his palace tonight.

BUTTERCUP: Delighted. I accept.

DAISY (*aside*): Once the Prince sees me, he'll want me as his wife. He'd be a fool not to.

BUTTERCUP (*aside*): As soon as the Prince sets his eyes on me and all my loveliness, he'll ask me

to marry him at once. He'd be mad if he didn't.

DAISY: I accept too.

PRINCE: Well, I'm glad you can both come. Now what about your younger sister?

BUTTERCUP: } What?
DAISY: }

PRINCE: Your younger sister.

BUTTERCUP: } Who?
DAISY: }

PRINCE: She is to be invited as well.

BUTTERCUP: But we haven't got a younger sister.

DAISY: Well, not so as you'd notice, anyway.

BUTTONS: Yes, they have and here she is!

(*Buttons steps forward and drags Cinderella with him. Prince Charming gasps.*)

PRINCE (*aside*): But she is beautiful! This is the girl I've dreamed of marrying.

BUTTONS: This is Baron Hardup's youngest daughter, Cinderella.

(*Cinderella curtsies.*)

PRINCE: Miss Cinderella, you too must come to the ball tonight. Prince Charming especially wishes it.

CINDERELLA: Thank you, kind sir.

PRINCE: Now, I must be on my way. I have all the great houses in the district still to visit. You must excuse me, ladies. Good day.

(*Prince Charming goes out the way he came in, followed by Buttons.*)

CINDERELLA: Invited to the ball, me? It's too good to be true.

BUTTERCUP: You're right there, child. Going to the ball's far too good for the likes of you.

DAISY: Yes, the Prince doesn't want an ordinary char at his party. He wants ladies of grace and refinement and exquisite beauty—like me!

BUTTERCUP: And me!

DAISY: Come on, sister, we must go and put on our ball gowns. If we're to be the belles of the ball, we'd better get to work right away.

BUTTERCUP: Back to work, Cinders. We're off to the ball.

(*Buttercup and Daisy go off to the left, leaving Cinderella alone.*)

CINDERELLA: Oh, I do so want to go to the Prince's ball, but how can I? I've got nothing to wear, but these rags. My sisters won't let me travel with them and it's far too far to walk. I thought it was too good to be true.

(*Cinderella sits by the fireside, dejected. The Fairy Godmother suddenly appears.*)

FAIRY GODMOTHER: Sweet Cinderella, have no fear—your Fairy Godmother is here.

CINDERELLA: Am I dreaming?

FAIRY GODMOTHER: Of course not, my dear. I'm sorry if I startled you. I've only come to help.

CINDERELLA: But how can you help?

FAIRY GODMOTHER: You want to go to the Prince's ball tonight?

CINDERELLA: Yes, but I've nothing to wear.

FAIRY GODMOTHER: Don't worry. My fairy power can turn those rags into the loveliest dress you ever saw. My magic wand will turn a pumpkin into a fairy carriage and small white mice into fine white horses. You *shall* go to the ball tonight!

CINDERELLA: Oh, thank you, thank you, thank you!

FAIRY GODMOTHER: One thing you must remember. At the stroke of midnight my fairy power ends and you must leave the ball by then or your coach and horses will disappear and your beautiful dress will turn back into rags.

CINDERELLA: I'll be good, I promise.

FAIRY GODMOTHER: Come Cinderella, come one and all, Let's make our way to the Prince's ball.

End of Scene One

Scene Two: THE BALLROOM AT THE PALACE

(*Buttercup and Daisy are with Prince Charming.*)

BUTTERCUP: Oh, Prince Charming, you are awful!
DAISY: But I like you.
BUTTERCUP: Fancy pretending to be your valet, Bebeano.
PRINCE: Dandini.
BUTTERCUP: That's what I meant. Fancy pretending to be your valet, Danbeano, when you were the Prince all the time.
DAISY: You are a one.
BUTTERCUP: Would you care for a dance, Your Highness?
DAISY: Yes, would you care for a dance?
BUTTERCUP: I asked first.
DAISY: Yes, but I'm prettier.
BUTTERCUP: Stuff and nonsense.
(*Prince Charming coughs.*)
PRINCE: Ladies, ladies, please!
DAISY: Forgive her, Prince Charming, she's ill-bred.
BUTTERCUP: Don't pay any attention to her, Your Highness. She can't help it you know.
DAISY: Poor dear, she's so old she's forgotten what manners are!
BUTTERCUP: Oh, I could bite you!
DAISY: Yes, you could—if you hadn't left your teeth at home! Ha! Ha!
PRINCE: Girls!
BUTTERCUP: }
DAISY: } Yes?
PRINCE: You're giving me a headache.
BUTTERCUP: }
DAISY: } Forgive her!

PRINCE: Perhaps you would be kind enough to fetch me a glass of water. I think it might do my headache good.

BUTTERCUP:
DAISY: } Of course, I'll get it!

BUTTERCUP: No, I'll get it.

DAISY: Let me get it. I have a way with water.

PRINCE: Why don't you both go and get it.

BUTTERCUP:
DAISY: } Oh, all right. Bye bye for now.

(*And off they go to get the Prince's water.*)

PRINCE: Alone, at last. Now to find that beautiful girl I danced with a few moments ago. Look, here she comes.

(*Enter Cinderella.*)

PRINCE: Fair lady, what is your name?

CINDERELLA: That is a secret, sir. What is yours?

PRINCE: I am Prince Charming.

CINDERELLA (*aside*): So he's not Dandini!

PRINCE: And I'd like you to be my Princess.

CINDERELLA: Oh, but Your Highness...

(*The clock begins to strike twelve.*)

PRINCE: Will you say yes?

CINDERELLA: I, I—

PRINCE: Yes?

CINDERELLA: I must fly!

(*She runs offstage as the clock strikes twelve.*)

PRINCE: Lady, sweet lady, come back!

(*Enter Buttercup and Daisy. Buttercup is carrying a glass of water. Daisy is carrying a glass slipper.*)

BUTTERCUP: } We're back.
DAISY: }

PRINCE: Did you pass anyone on the way?

BUTTERCUP: As a matter of fact we did. Some sort of serving girl. She almost knocked me over.

DAISY: Rude thing!

BUTTERCUP: Never mind, I've brought you your glass of water.

DAISY: And I've brought you this glass slipper. We found it on the way.

PRINCE: *Her* slipper! Give it to me. I shall search the land, I shall search the world, and whoever's foot shall fit this glass slipper shall be my bride.

BUTTERCUP: Well, this is quite a turn-up for the books.

DAISY: The Prince falling for a slipper and ignoring our good looks.

End of Scene Two

Scene Three: THE KITCHEN AT STONYBROKE HALL

(*Cinderella and Buttons are discovered by the fireside.*)

BUTTONS: Well, Cinders, did you have a good time last night?

CINDERELLA: Oh, I did, Buttons, I did.

BUTTONS: Did you meet Prince Charming?

CINDERELLA: I did, and you'll never believe it, but he asked me to marry him.

BUTTONS: He didn't.

CINDERELLA: He did.

BUTTONS: And did you say 'Yes'?

CINDERELLA: No.

BUTTONS: Phew! That's a relief, because you know, Cinders, I want to marry you myself.

CINDERELLA: But I didn't say 'No'.

(*There is a knock at the door.*)

BUTTONS: I'd better go.

(*Buttons goes to answer the door and Buttercup and Daisy enter from the other direction.*)

BUTTERCUP: Standing about doing nothing, as usual, I see.

DAISY: I don't know who you think you are, Cinderella. Lady Muck? You can't spend all day every day idling about.

BUTTERCUP: Go and get on with your work, child.

DAISY: Go on! Shoo!

(*Cinderella goes off.*)

BUTTERCUP: Oh, she's a lazy girl.

DAISY: Dreadful. If only she wasn't our sister, we could give her the sack.

(*Enter Buttons and Prince Charming.*)

BUTTONS: His Royal Highness, Prince Charming.

PRINCE: Good morning, ladies.

BUTTERCUP: How sweet of you to call Prince Charming.

DAISY: The answer's 'Yes', by the way, Prince Charming.

PRINCE: Yes—what?

DAISY: Yes. I will marry you.

BUTTERCUP: Oh no you won't.

DAISY: Oh, yes I will.

BUTTERCUP: Oh, no you won't.

DAISY: Oh, yes I will.

PRINCE: Ladies, please.

BUTTONS: Belt up!

PRINCE: I *will* marry one of you—

BUTTERCUP: }
DAISY: } Oh!

PRINCE: *If* this slipper fits.

DAISY: Don't worry, it will.

BUTTERCUP: Hand it over, I'll try it on first.

DAISY: No you won't, I'll go first.

BUTTERCUP: *Me* first!

BUTTONS: Prince Charming, why don't you let the *older* of the two sisters try it on first?

PRINCE: What a good idea. Which one of you should be first?

DAISY: Not me, Your Highness, not me.

BUTTERCUP: Of course, it should be her. She's years and *years* older than I am. I'm a mere child.

DAISY: You're an old fossil!

PRINCE: Now stop arguing and come over here.

(*Daisy goes to the Prince who kneels down and tries to fit the slipper onto her right foot.*)

DAISY: It fits, it fits!

PRINCE: What do you mean 'It fits!'? I can't even get your toes in, never mind your heel.

DAISY: Well, I didn't want to marry you anyway.
BUTTERCUP: Sour grapes. Well, sister, watch me.
(*Buttercup goes to the Prince who tries to fit the slipper onto her foot.*)
BUTTERCUP: Ow!
PRINCE: What's the matter?
BUTTERCUP: I've got warts on the ends of my toes!
PRINCE: Warts or no warts, the slipper doesn't fit.
BUTTERCUP: Silly slipper.
PRINCE: Are there any other ladies in the house?
DAISY: We're the only ones.
PRINCE: Are you sure?
BUTTERCUP: } Yes!
DAISY: }
BUTTONS: They're lying, Your Highness.
BUTTERCUP: } Oh no we're not.
DAISY: }
BUTTONS: Oh yes you are—and I'll prove it.
(*Buttons rushes off.*)
BUTTERCUP: Cheeky scamp.
DAISY: Impudent rascal.
(*Buttons returns with Cinderella.*)
BUTTONS: Your Highness, this is Cinderella.
PRINCE: I think we've met before. Cinderella, let me see if this glass slipper fits you, because if it does I will ask you to be my bride.
(*The Prince kneels at Cinderella's feet and tries on the slipper.*)
PRINCE: It fits!
BUTTONS: Hooray!
BUTTERCUP: } Boo!
DAISY: }
PRINCE: Cinderella, will you be mine?
CINDERELLA: Dear Prince Charming, I will.
BUTTERCUP: Well, I knew he had no taste.

DAISY: I can't see what he sees in a walking scarecrow like her. She's not fit to be a princess. It's ridiculous.

BUTTONS: Congratulations, Cinderella. I'm so pleased you are going to be happy at last. You deserve all the happiness in the whole wide world.

CINDERELLA: Oh, thank you Buttons, you're the best friend a girl could have.

BUTTONS: I hope you'll live happily ever after.

CINDERELLA: But Buttons you must come and live with us at the palace.

BUTTERCUP: }
DAISY: } Can we come too?

CINDERELLA: Can they, Prince?

PRINCE: If they promise to be good.

BUTTERCUP: }
DAISY: } We do

CINDERELLA: So we'll *all* live happily ever after.

PRINCE:

The story's ended happily and now's the time
To bring the curtain down on Inman's pantomime.
Let's go and sing and dance and cheer and shout 'Hooray!'
For this is now fair Cinderella's Wedding Day!

The Show Must Go On

Whatever sort of show you're putting on—whether it's a pantomime or Punch and Judy, a concert party or a costume parade—you will usually find your audience is 'with you', wanting everything to go well, so that they enjoy themselves and can see that you're enjoying yourselves, too. Sometimes, though, things will go wrong. If the audience is made up of young children, they will lose interest in the show unless there's something fresh happening all the time. If this seems to be the case and you notice they're rustling sweet papers and staring at the floor more than the stage, there are two things you can do.

The first is to involve them. Get them to join in with the clowns, or to shout out what they think the shadow is supposed to be on the screen, or to sing along with a nursery rhyme. Or, you can change your act. This sounds dramatic, but it really means just doing the things that the youngest will enjoy. If you're performing a card trick they may not be able to follow, try the banana trick instead. They'll be so amazed at this piece of 'real magic' that they'll make a bigger effort to concentrate.

If you're in the middle of a play, you won't, of course, be able to change the script or start singing 'Baa-baa Black Sheep'. The only thing to do is not have too many young children in the audience!

You may find that older people misbehave, too! As they're at home, they may drop off to sleep or chatter. If they do, make a loud bang; not so loud that you give your Granny a heart-attack, but just enough to get their attention. Adults are really just big children, and instead of doing what they tell *you* to do, they do what they tell you not to do, and not only that, they do it more loudly than you would!

Don't be *too* hard on them. They may be enjoying the show very much even though they look as if they're dozing!

Your friends may act differently. If they're in the audience and feeling a bit jealous because they're not on-stage, they may think it's funny to shout at you while you're singing or acting. What they don't realise is that you're going to ask them to come on to the stage and repeat what they were saying so everyone can hear them better! Most people will shut up once they have been asked on-stage, but some may accept and walk up. When they get to the stage, or into the arena, they will find that suddenly, they're not so sure of themselves. The stage is a lonely place when you aren't sure of your lines, and they will now be facing the audience instead of being part of it. Even if they do manage to splutter out what they said, everyone will be bored with them and be more eager than before to watch the show.

Interruptions like this can often be a help rather than a disaster. It gives you a chance to get closer to the audience, and to get them on your side by making fun of someone who's trying to be clever.

This will work if one of the audience interrupts your circus, but it won't be the answer if he interrupts you when you're doing some magic. The magic may not be going very well, so if someone is shouting out 'Seen it before!' or 'That's not very clever!' or 'My dog can do better tricks than that!', it's a great chance for you to show how good you are.

Say you are going to ask him to do something very simple—it's not even a trick—and if he can do it, you will give him £5! He'll probably accept the challenge.

Place a stool against a wall and ask Mister Smart Alec to face the wall in front of the stool, with his feet together. Tell him to stand so his toes are roughly twice the width of the stool away from the wall.

Now ask him to lean forward, and, holding the sides of the stool, rest his head against the wall. All he has to do to win £5 is to lift the stool off the floor and stand upright. You can tease him as much as you like, he won't be able to do it. He will go back to his seat and, if he has any sense, will clap loudly when you finish.

If you dry up during any other sort of show, it's a good idea to have a bit of verse ready. Just suppose that in the middle of your shadow show, the torch bulb goes. You should have another torch ready in case that happens, but just pretend that you've forgotten about that. What do you do? You can turn on the light, but what then? If you leave the audience and go off and find another torch or table lamp, they'll get fidgety, and the whole thing will seem a bit poor. Learn a few limericks or funny stories. Then, while one of you goes off to find another light, the other can keep the entertainment going with such classic pieces of literature as:

There was a young fellow named Saul,
  Who went to a Fancy Dress Ball;
He thought he could risk it
  And go as a biscuit,
But a dog ate him up in the hall!

It doesn't matter what you recite as long as it raises a smile.

Usually the audience will be more than eager for you to succeed. As long as they enjoy the show, it doesn't matter that a few things go wrong.

If getting started is difficult for you, it's nearly as difficult deciding where to finish. Remember that the audience will get tired of watching before you get tired of acting or singing, no matter how good you are.

When you plan your show, don't do as much as you would enjoy; pretend you're in the audience. If it seems to drag, cut bits out, re-write the sections where nothing much happens. The audience should be glad to see the show, but they shouldn't be glad to see the end of it! If it's good, and of the right

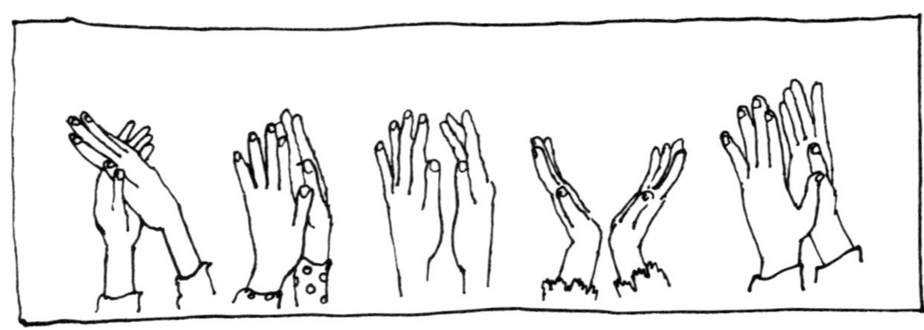

length, they should be left wanting more. You must make it clear that the last trick you do, or the last act you have on the stage, *is* the last one so they know when to applaud, and when to get up and go!

If you leave everyone happy, the show will be remembered as a good show and when you ask them if they can come to the next one, they'll all shout enthusiastically, 'I'm free!'

Good luck!